DRAGON

Rhayader

To Lou

Alan Davenport

DRAGON POTTERY
Rhayader

Its History and Products

Alan G Davenport

DRAGON POTTERY

Published in Great Britain in 2005 by
Alan G Davenport
11 Wallcroft
Willaston
NESTON CH64 2UE

A catalogue record for this book is available from
the British Library.

ISBN 0-9549660-0-7
ISBN 978-0-9549660-0-3

Designed and typeset by the author

Printed and bound in Great Britain by
WH Evans & Sons Ltd.
5 Knutsford Way
Sealand Industrial Estate
Chester CH1 4NS

Contents

Acknowledgements

I would like to thank Mrs D Cornish, Mr Tom Griffiths, Mrs Ann Pugh(nee Thomas), Mrs Jill Fenner, Mr Aubrey Thomas, Mr Philip Lumsden, Mrs Christine Harris(nee Nicholls), and Mrs Val Evans, for giving their time to be interviewed, and permitting me to photograph, and publish, items of pottery in their possession, together with the loan of photographs and newspaper cuttings. For privacy reasons I have not identified these items with their owners.

I would also like to take this opportunity to thank all those users of the Ebay auction site, on the Internet, who have given permission for their photographs to be used to supplement those from my own collection. In the very few instances where no reply was received to the request it is anticipated that no objection was raised. Recognition of all copyright is given by showing their Ebay 'user-name' with the appropriate photograph(s).

My thanks are also given to Mr Peter Saunders OBE, Chairman and Managing Director of Halo Foods Ltd, Tywyn, for information relating to the design, and use, of Dragon products in the packaging of honey, which was produced by Holgate Honey Farm of Aberaeron. This was the company which he joined as a production manager in 1975 and purchased, except for the ice cream business, in October 1976.

Introduction

My reason for writing this book was that, as a small collector, I was extremely frustrated, and infuriated, in not being able to find any reliable, or authoritative, information in books, magazines, or on the Internet, about when the pottery operated or correct descriptions for the products. An enquiry to the National Museums and Galleries of Wales, in June 1999, drew a blank with the added statement "likely to be fairly recent date (? within the last thirty years)".

My initial thoughts were that, 20 years after the company was forced into liquidation, there would be little likelihood of finding any reliable information locally.

Eventually, as a result of searching the Internet I did manage to contact Phil Rogers, who is the local studio potter in Rhayader, and a young lady by the name of Dee who was involved with the www.britisharchives.co.uk website, also in Rhayader. Both told me that Mrs Cornish still lived in the Rhayader area. Armed with this information, I was able to contact Mrs Cornish, an original founder, who agreed to give me my first interview at which she gave her approval and to be of help in my quest for more information.

Immediately following this interview I contacted Mrs Val Evans, Secretary of Rhayader Women's Institute, who was kind enough to enquire if any of the members were former employees. Unfortunately, there was none but the Press Officer, who unbeknown to me, passed my details to the local newspaper. A couple of weeks later I received a number of telephone calls, which meant that my research could begin in earnest.

It has not been an easy task to gather the data as there would appear to be no surviving records of product designs, nor styles of decoration, and that no illustrated catalogues were ever produced.

Each of my initial interviews has taken place in the interviewee's own home, followed by an occasional telephone call at a later date.

Over 40 years have passed since production started so most those who were interviewed, who were only in their late teens at the time, are now in their mid to late fifties. Memories tend to fade with time, and age, and this was no exception, but fortunately I was able to support my interviews with the stimulation of a comprehensive set of photographs which proved so helpful that most interviews took a lot longer than anticipated due to the fact that memories were rekindled and the information and stories started to flow.

Most dates are only approximations but a few are accurate: -

a) 1962 – start of production.
b) November 1963 and March 1964 – newspaper articles.
c) 1978 (late) – Sale of business to Mr E Husson.
d) 1982 (late summer) – ceased trading – liquidation sale of assets.
e) Items produced to commemorate local events, etc.

The main sources of information used in compiling this publication were: -

a) Interviews with Mrs Cornish, who was a founder with her husband, and with some of the former employees who had a reasonable length of service with the company.

b) Studying the items in my own collection and in the possession of those interviewed.

c) Observing the items that have appeared on the Ebay auction site on the Internet.

d) Reports in the local newspaper, The Times Gazette, dated 28th November 1963, 5th March 1964 and others.

The few personal details relating to Mr and Mrs Cornish have previously been published in the local press. This was at the time that Mr Cornish was being interviewed as part of the campaign to obtain planning permission for the new factory and bungalow.

It must be appreciated that this publication is not a complete account of the history of Dragon Pottery, and its products, but it is the best that could be produced with the information available.

If any reader has any additional information, recollections, or more accurate information, then I will be delighted to record the facts so that they can be placed on file and included in any later edition.

Similarly, if any reader can supply a photograph of any item, either pot or style of decoration, which has not been featured then I would, again, be delighted to receive it, preferably digitally via e-mail, so that it can be placed on record for future reference.

It must be clearly stated that Dragon Pottery, of Rhayader, has never been associated with any other pottery that has used the name 'Dragon', nor has it ever been associated with any other pottery in Rhayader, the Elan Valley, or anywhere else.

Finally, it is hoped that this publication will place the achievements of Dragon Pottery on record and into the history of Rhayader and the Welsh pottery industry for present and future generations, and to clear any misunderstanding about when the pottery operated, how the products were made, and the descriptive names given to the products.

Alan G Davenport
Willaston, 2005

Email dragonpottery@btinternet.com

The Formative Years

The foundations for Dragon Pottery, Rhayader, were laid in the early 1950's when Mr and Mrs Cornish carried on in business selling hardware, and giftware, from two shops in the town. One shop was in North Street, under the name of C & M Stores, and the other was the very old black and white half-timbered building on the corner of South Street and East Street.

It was during these early days that they had the idea of making souvenir ashtrays, in the shape of one of the Elan Valley dams, using plaster of Paris. This venture proved so popular with the tourists that Mr Cornish decided he would like to try his hand at craft pottery. As a result of this both he, and Mrs Cornish, enrolled at local evening classes to learn the basic craft skills required, and determine which items of equipment would be needed to set up a small production unit.

Mr Robert Cornish, who was a Master Builder, was no stranger to the world of clay. He was born in Wickford, Essex, where he joined the family brick manufacturing business, and at the outbreak of World War II he moved to Birmingham where he was involved with the local Civil Defence.

After the war Mr Cornish took a day trip into Central Wales. He liked the area so much that he decided to look for a place to live and settle down. Rhayader was his choice and it was here that he met his wife to be, Miss Doreen Morgan, whose home was at Llanwrthwl, only four miles away.

Into Production

Towards the end of 1961, or perhaps early 1962, and after only a few lessons at the evening class, Mr Cornish decided that he had gained sufficient knowledge to be able to start production on a very small scale. A potter's wheel, a small kiln, and a supply of china clay, was obtained so that a small production unit could be set up in the cellar of the property where they were living at the time. This property was known as 'Somerset House' and was a former fish and chip shop on the corner of East Street and Caerherbert Lane in Rhayader.

Initially the pottery, and its products, was known by the name “Rhaeadr Gwy Pottery”. It was very soon realised, however, that a more powerful name was required to achieve wider recognition in the very competitive pottery and giftware market and so it was changed to “Dragon Pottery - Rhayader”, a name which was much easier to remember, and yet retain its name association with Wales. ‘Dragon Pottery’ was not registered as a limited liability company but was a business name used by Mr and Mrs Cornish. The name 'Red Dragon Pottery' was erroneously quoted in a newspaper article in November 1963 and, as a result of this, has been used by a few writers since.

Production was slow to begin with, due to the learning curve involved in building up the skills required to produce items with consistently good quality, and the fact that this was almost a one-man operation at the time.

It soon became apparent, however, that additional help was urgently required. To this end, an advertisement was placed in the Birmingham press with the result that the services of a student, by the name of Miss Carol Lawton, aged about 18 and from the Birmingham Art School, was obtained. Although Miss Lawton had little experience of ‘throwing’ clay on a wheel she, like Mr Cornish, had the aptitude to be able to learn a skill very quickly.

As soon as some designs of pots, and decoration, had been established, production really got under way during 1962. More staff were required and were recruited locally. All needed training, as no other similar work had been available in the area from which experience could be drawn.

The main requirement was for female labour with an artistic flair, or with a hidden artistic flair that could be developed with training. It was Mr Cornish, himself, who provided this initial training which was then developed further by actual experience, under constant expert supervision, as part of the workforce.

Some female staff worked a full week, some part-time days, and some in the evenings. Schoolgirls were often employed for a few hours in the evening. This gave Mr Cornish the opportunity to discover any artistic talent, which might be looking for employment in the not too distant future.

LIGHT INDUSTRY MAY HAVE TO LEAVE AREA

Rhayader firm's difficulty in need for expansion

A GROWING light industry in Rhayader may be forced to leave the town, the county of Radnorshire, and perhaps Wales, unless it can find new and larger accommodation within the next twelve months.

The "Red Dragon" Pottery concern was started four years ago by a husband and wife team in a converted fish and chip shop in Caerherbert Lane, East Street, Rhayader. The idea was to market fancy pottery wares [illegible]

Pottery firm may be forced to move

Planning Permission

As time progressed and demand, and production, increased it became obvious, early in 1963, that premises, larger than the converted fish and chip shop, would be required. The staffing level had risen to about eight and the production area was not just in the original cellar, but upstairs in rooms at pavement level, in the lean-to extension on the side of the property, and in an out-house at the rear.

By this time, most likely, at least three small kilns, and one medium kiln, had been installed.

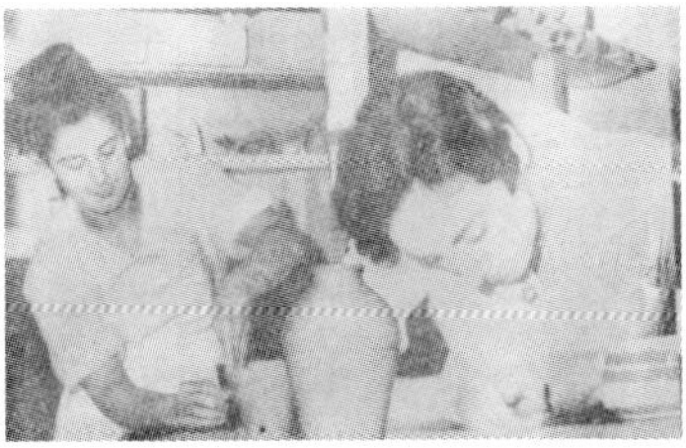

Some of the workers at Mr and Mrs Cornish's Pottery in Rhayader. From the left they are: Nineteen-year-old Carol Lawton, a product of Birmingham art school and college; Ann Thomas, 18, from Llanwrthwl, who "thinks of everything" about the pottery; asbestos-gloved Veronica Dowding, 18, removing hot "pots" from one of the small kilns with 16-year-old Philip Lumsden; Mrs Jill Fenner and Phyllis Hedges hand-painting designs.

Times Gazette 28th November 1963

An application had been made to the local council for permission to develop an area of land on the local industrial estate for a new building to house all of the production facilities. Permission had also been requested to build a bungalow, on the same site, as a residence for Mr and Mrs Cornish. The requirement for the bungalow was so that Mr Cornish could be on hand to attend to the kilns during the night. These kilns were heated electrically and used the overnight electricity tariff, not only to keep costs down but also that not too great a strain would be placed on the local electricity supply network, which was not as robust as it is today.

Needless to say, the application was rejected by the local council because of the residential element. As a result of this decision, Mr Cornish started a publicity campaign to gain support not only from the local population but also from the County Council and the Welsh Development Agency. The local newspaper, The Times Gazette, carried a large article on the matter in their edition dated 28th November, 1963.

Eventually, as a result of this and other local representations, planning permission was finally granted, but not before production was brought to a stand-still for many weeks due to a serious fire in the kiln room in the original premises. This fire was fully reported in the local newspaper dated 5th March, 1964.

The New Pottery

The new pottery, a sectional pre-cast concrete building with an asbestos roof, and the brick bungalow known as 'Sunnyside', were finally erected on the industrial estate at the easterly end of East Street.

The date of the completion of the new premises is a little unclear, but is likely to have been towards the spring of 1965, with full production being transferred during the first part of 1966. Production could then be increased and eventually up to about twenty staff were employed.

Staff recruitment was always an ongoing problem especially with the move into the new building and the need for more staff.

During the eight or nine years in which pots were made on the wheel there only appears to have been three main potters employed in this period. One or two others did spend a little time 'throwing' before taking up other duties within the pottery.

On the decorating side there was a fairly high turnover of female staff but, luckily, a small number was very loyal and with some impressive years of service to their credit even though a few did have breaks in order to raise families.

Supporting the potters, and decorating staff, there was a small number of devoted employees to keep the supply of clay and moulds flowing and to look after the kilns during the time when the pots were being fired.

The firing capacity was increased to four small kilns, two medium kilns, and two trolley kilns.

From the time that all of the production had been transferred to the new pottery, and the increased firing capacity installed, very little changed although new pot designs and decorative patterns were introduced from time to time. In about 1971, the process of 'throwing' was abandoned in favour of the 'slipcast' method of production, which had started, in a small way ,in late 1964.

Coach tour operators very soon realised that the pottery was in production and were not slow to include it in the itinerary for their tours in the area. At the peak of the summer season, it was not unknown for as many as eight coaches to arrive during the day. Some tour companies notified their visit in advance but others just ‘arrived’. Mrs Cornish was usually on hand to provide a conducted tour for each party.

In 1978 Mr and Mrs Cornish decided to retire and sell the pottery business.

Towards the end of that year Mr Ernest Husson, who already owned a well established photographic business in Llandrindod Wells, purchased the business and formed a limited company, ‘Dragon Pottery Limited’, Company No. 1404122, with Mr Husson, and his wife, as directors.

In 1979 Mr Husson became the youngest-ever president of the Welsh National Chamber of Trade, and the first one to come from Mid-Wales.

After Mr Ernest Husson took over the business a small temporary building was erected which was used as a snack bar for the visiting tourists.

Sadly, in about September 1982, Mr Husson was forced into liquidation, the pottery and company closed down, and all the assets sold off. The company was finally officially dissolved on 11th March 1985.

Since the closure a haulage contractor and perhaps others have used the building. At the time of writing, 2005, the building is in a poor state of repair with some of the panels missing from the westerly end of the roof.

DRAGON POTTERY
MADE
IN
WALES
RHAYADER

Sales

Most of the production from Dragon carried the brand 'Dragon Pottery – Rhayader – Made in Wales' stamped on the base.

Retail sales were made from the two shops in Rhayader, through freelance sales representatives, wholesalers, and by Mrs Cornish filling the van with stock and travelling around Wales and the West Midlands selling to any likely outlets. The 'Ovenware' range was sold mainly through departmental stores in London.

Sales through freelance sales representatives were disappointing, and at least one wholesaler in North Wales ceased trading, leaving a rather large amount of unpaid debt outstanding.

In about 1965, a very good trading relationship was developed between Dragon and a company known as 'Dee Cee'. This relationship appears to have lasted into the 1970's.

Desmond Cooper, who traded under the name of 'Dee Cee', was an importer/wholesaler from the Birmingham area. Dee Cee, amongst other things, marketed pottery products under its own name, having obtained them from various potteries both in the UK and in Europe. The company took large quantities of standard Dragon pots but decorated to its own specification and stamped 'Dee Cee – Made in Wales'.

Several pottery marketing companies, and specialised outlets, took standard Dragon ranges decorated with their own designs and with the Dragon stamp on the base. One, or two, provided their own product design for Dragon to manufacture and decorate. A company known as Charles Gordon, which manufactured mustard, chutney and sauces, and which had strong connections with a delicatessen in Bridgnorth, was one such company, although no further details are available.

Some pots were designed specifically for a customer but still carried the Dragon stamp. One instance of this was Holgate Honey, of Aberaeron, which had two designs made for them. In another instance a small pot, like a very small marmalade pot, was designed, and made, for another Welsh honey company of which no further details are known. Photographs of all three designs have been included in the Product Gallery.

Throughout the life of Dragon, there was always the willingness to incorporate a place name, a commercial name, the commemoration of an event, or anything of that nature, into the decoration in an attempt to promote the name of Dragon and increase sales.

Product Decoration

The success of Dragon can be attributed to the good business acumen and artistic talent possessed by Mr and Mrs Cornish in having an attractive style of decoration on an attractive design of pottery at a reasonable price.

The style of decoration, which was established when production of thrown pots was first started in 1962, was based on numerous bands of autumn colours around the outside of the pot. Each band of colour being separated by a very shallow plain white band, and each colour band containing a different etched design.

For the first twelve months, these designs were mainly based on the intense use of straight lines.

As ideas were developed the next period, from late 1963, saw the introduction of curves into the range of designs while those designs which featured the use of straight lines were gradually reduced.

Eventually, over the period 1964/65, the range of etched designs was completely reviewed. It was decided to introduce designs, which were more simple and less intense.

Most of these new designs were more 'outline' in character and thus revealed more of the background colour than previously. Some were based on forms of leaf depicted as single leaves, sprigs of leaves and creepers. Others were based on scrollwork, which can be found on many ancient artefacts from the eastern Mediterranean and other countries. Some were based on comb effects, and others were designed, and developed, by some of the employees themselves.

The first few of these designs were, most likely, used in late 1964 when the first slipcast 'Salt and Pepper' were produced.

At the same time as these new designs were introduced changes were made to reduce the number of colour bands and to make them deeper.

Most of the pots that were thrown and used the new designs, together with early pots that were slipcast, featured a shallow band of a dark colour, usually black or brown, in the centre of the white separating band.

After a short time this dark shallow band was given a yellow background that gave the pots a new bright look.

From about 1966, when slipcast production started to get under way, and replace the thrown method, these new designs were applied to all of the Dragon brand production as well as to all other new pot designs when they were introduced.

This new range of designs was so successful that it lasted in production until the end of Dragon in 1982.

Some time during 1965 Dragon agreed to supply Dee Cee with pots of its choice and decorated to its own specifications.

Dee Cee took virtually all of the range, which was thrown, and specified that only black bands of colour should be used. These to be decorated with designs that were already being applied to standard Dragon production. The 'Black' Range was extended to most of the slipcast pots as they became available.

When the new cruet set was introduced, Dee Cee also took this in black, but only for a short time, before introducing its own distinctive 'Brown Leaf' design to it, and to the rest of the product range being taken. The 'Black' slipcast range continued alongside the 'Brown Leaf' range up to about 1970.

In about 1967 a small range, featuring a brown leaf, and sometimes a green leaf, was developed where there were deep bands of brown and green separated by shallow bands of white and yellow. The leaf was enhanced by having its outline, and veins, highlighted by careful use of the etching tool. Very few examples of this range have been observed, just several jugs, a pot with a lid, and a table lamp in a private collection. These items are stamped Dragon. Dragon ceased to use the leaf, in either colour, when Dee Cee adopted the brown leaf design on the green background for his range from early 1968.

The basis of the Dee Cee brown leaf design was usually a fairly shallow band of brown at the top of the pot, which featured one of the long linked etched designs. The remainder of the pot consisted of green bands over which the leaf was painted. A few pots featured only one band of green but most featured several.

In the late 1960's Dee Cee also took most of the range of pots with the usual Dragon style of decoration but using just black and light brown instead of the autumn colours. The etched decoration was usually only applied to the deep black band.

After the production of slipcast pots was firmly established, other new styles of decoration were introduced in an attempt to increase sales further.

In late 1960's trials were made using lustre glaze without any other form of decoration. One of these was bright, like silver, and the other was dark, like gunmetal. They appear to have only been applied to a small range.

A small range of vases featuring two bands of brown and incorporating holiday resort place names was tried, in about 1968, but with limited success.

In 1969 most of the pots designs were incorporated into a range in which the only colour used was blue. Some were decorated in one deep band and others with two bands, one being of greater depth than the other. Some were produced without the etched design and some with it, in either the upper or both bands. This range was reasonably successful, from a sales point of view, but there were production problems in that it was very difficult to maintain a good quality of colour, and the colour tended to bubble under the glaze when fired. It was re-launched in 1972 for a short period.

1971 saw a change in the grade/quality of the clay being used. This produced a cream coloured pot although it did vary, from time to time, between 'almost white' and 'rich cream'.

The 1970's saw numerous attempts to increase sales with the introduction of various new colour schemes.

It was during this period that a mottled, or marbled, effect was applied to most of the product range. Details of this decorating technique can be found in the Production Processes chapter.

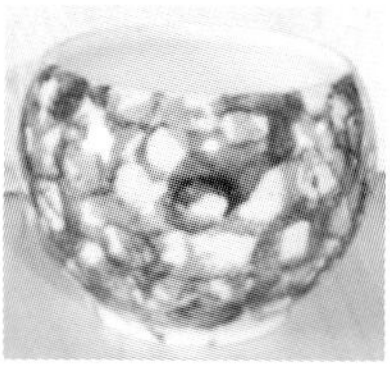

In 1973, or a little later, a range with bands of brown, separated by shallow bands of yellow, was applied to most of the pots.

Another was the Rainbow Range, which featured many shallow bands of various colours, some of which had not been used before.

Other colour ranges, which were produced in the 1970's, included one in an overall mustard colour and which was applied to most of the kitchen and tableware designs. Another range featured the use of broad brush strokes using pale green, brown and yellow applied to items of tableware.

Again, in the mid 1970's, a demand was identified for a cheaper, but still colourful, product. This was met by taking the standard Dragon autumn tints bands of colour but without the etched decoration. This style was applied to most of the range that was current at the time.

In 1978 the business was sold to Mr Husson who, besides still producing most of the traditional Dragon designs, entered the souvenir market with transfers being applied to mugs, or more correctly tankards. This was at the time of the build-up to the royal wedding when many producers were offering Charles and Diana items with Dragon becoming one of them.

As well as the royal wedding souvenir mugs Mr Husson also produced souvenir mugs for the tourist market featuring Welsh themes, and even produced one featuring a map of Cornwall for their tourist industry. He also produced a large number of mugs featuring various nursery rhymes for children, as well as themes from childrens' TV.

Product Range Development

Mr Cornish enjoyed working on the wheel with clay and over the years, many new designs were evolved. Among these were table lamps, vases, marmalade pots, jugs, mugs, fruit dishes, various other small dishes, each in various shapes and sizes.

The early range of thrown pots was very modest and allowed both the potters and artists to gain experience at their new craft. It also allowed time for an assessment to be made of the market demand for the products.

The photograph on the left, from the local newspaper, dated 28th November 1963, gives a good indication of the pot designs that were being made at the time showing small bowls, plant pots, plain and flask shaped vases and the first design of table lamp in a shape not unlike that of a 'Tia Maria' bottle.

In about 1964, the design of the small bowl was changed to one that was more round and bulbous. This was at the time when the style of the etched designs was revised to the one that introduced curves, in various forms, and featured less use of straight lines.

It is thought that Dragon first used the slipcast method, on a very small scale, in the old premises towards the end of 1964.

The first design of pot to be produced by this method was most likely the 'slim-line' 'Salt and Pepper', which was 5½" tall, ⅝" across the top, and 2" across the base. It featured five colour bands incorporating the new style of etched patterns.

Space is a major requirement where slipcasting is carried out and it was not until the new spacious premises were available, some time in 1965, that slipcasting really started to get under way.

Prior to the move into the new premises all the plant pots, and their associated saucers, were produced by the thrown method. After the move to the new premises a pug mill, and a press, were installed. The installation of the pug mill meant that the waste clay could be recycled and used in the press to produce plant pots and saucers, further details of which can be found in the Product Process chapter.

New pots were still being designed to be thrown and in about 1965, Dragon started to produce a new range of vases and fruit dishes. A new design of table lamp, known as the 'Beehive', was also introduced together with one or two variations.

After slipcast production got under way in the new premises, very little new happened with thrown pot designs other than the application of revised styles of decoration.

Production of thrown pots was gradually phased out as new moulds for the slipcast versions became available. 1971 saw the end of thrown pot production although it is extremely likely that Mr Cornish used the wheel, occasionally, to experiment with different ideas, or to make master models prior to making the plaster moulds ready for slipcast production.

The demands on production meant that the changeover to the slipcast method be carried out as quickly as possible. This was also the time to introduce new designs that were not feasible with the thrown method. It also meant that some designs, which were previously thrown, could be made with thinner walls and so create a small saving in the amount of clay used. Slipcasting also meant that pots of a more consistant size, and shape, could be produced in larger numbers.

A new Cruet Set comprising Salt, Pepper, Vinegar, and Mustard Pot was introduced at a very early stage, perhaps late 1965. The 'Salt and Pepper' was of more bold proportions than the one that it replaced.

Although the Vinegar and Mustard Pot remained virtually unchanged during the whole time that they were in production the 'Salt and Pepper' saw various mould sizes being used, 6", 5½", 5", and eventually a 3" version, although this last one was sold as a pair and not part of the Cruet Set.

1965/6 saw the introduction of the Tea Pot, Tea Pot Stand, and Coffee Pot. Although a cup, which it was claimed was Dragon, has appeared on the Internet none of the former employees, who were interviewed, can recall such a product.

A set of dishes was produced in late 1969. So far, only two Steak Dishes (7 x 4) have been observed. They are oval in shape with a very prominent footring and are white with a decoration, in black, not seen previously, or since, on any item of Dragon pottery. It is thought that they were given to employees as a Christmas present.

Planters, i.e. plant pots without the hole, were introduced in the late 1960's, the first ones having plain sloping sides. They were made in two sizes, 7½" and 4½" tall. A few years later, they were supplemented by a 4¾", and a 5½", each featuring a heavy upper rim. Another, 4½" tall, with a fluted rim was also introduced at about the same time.

A smaller version of the Thistle Vase, and Barrel Vase, was introduced. The Marmalade Pot and Butter Dish were remodelled with rounder edges and made slightly smaller. After a little while a demand for an even smaller Marmalade Pot was met with the introduction of the 3" model to supplement the 4" then currently in production.

The thrown Beehive Table Lamp, and Fruit Dish, were very popular items so master models, for the moulds, were made directly from actual examples of thrown production in order that a realistic impression of the potter's marks could be retained wherever possible.

The slipcast Beehive Table Lamp is so authentic that one needs to examine the inside of the pot to determine whether it was thrown or slipcast. Some of the examples that I have examined have had a 2" opening in the base through which it is an easy matter to see if the inside is rough or smooth, otherwise it is necessary to remove any light fitting which might be present. A rough inside indicates that it has been thrown, and a smooth inside that it was slipcast.

The outside of the slipcast Fruit Dish is also very authentic but the inside is smooth. The thickness of the slipcast version is usually slightly thicker. Production difficulties were sometimes encountered with this dish in that if the clay was too wet then the dish would collapse due to the softness, and the weight, of the clay forming the unsupported outer edges.

Four shapes of thrown jugs have been recorded, although there may be more. One is quite unusual in shape and the others quite conventional, and heavy, although small enough to be used for sauce at the dining table.

The slipcast Jug which was put into general production was of a traditional shape and was cast in two parts, the body and the handle. It has been related that it was Mrs Cornish who usually attached the handle to the body. Eventually the mould for the Jug was modified so that the body and handle were cast as one. Several sizes of slipcast jugs were made namely 3", 4", 5", and, possibly, 7½".

As well as the above jugs at least two styles were made for the little-known ovenware range. These are slightly larger, slipcast, but with the handle being attached rather than being cast as part of the total jug.

Several small dishes were made by the thrown method and did not present any problems when slipcast. These dishes were generally about 4" in diameter across the top and 3¼" across the base. Those that were slightly fluted were usually called Trinket or Pin Dishes and those that were heavily fluted were called Ashtrays. A plain dish with a small handle attached to the side was known as a Jam Dish.

A larger dish was added to the range from about 1970. This was 4" diameter across the base, 5½" across the top and 2" deep. Officially, this was known as a Bon Bon Dish, but some people have been known to use them as soup bowls.

The Small Round Bowl was another pot that was successfully converted to be slipcast. Several variations were made, slightly taller and with and without a lid, without a lid but with holes on the side and called a crocus bowl, and with a lid with holes called a small Rose Bowl. The large Rose Bowl was basically the Bulb Bowl modified to take a lid with holes.

At the end of the 1960's an Ovenware Range, not easily recognised as Dragon, was supplied to a number of London departmental stores. This range included ramekins, soufflé dishes, casserole dishes and heavy jugs.

Also, at about the same time, and again for London, a 'boat', and a special bowl incorporating a cube shaped base, were produced. Three versions of the boat, in two sizes, were supplied, dark blue, green, and white. The bowl has only been observed in silver lustre.

The following photograph of the storage area in the pottery clearly shows these two products drying out on the shelves prior to being biscuit fired. Photographs of the finished products are included in the Product Gallery.

The Drinking Mug has seen quite a change. The original designs were thrown, very plain, straight sided, and seemed to lack character. In about 1970 a slipcast, bulbous, style of Drinking Mug, with a large handle, was introduced for a short period and it was not until 1979, after Mr Husson purchased the pottery, that a replacement for this was introduced. This was in the shape of a tankard, although most people still refer to it as a mug.

In about 1971, the Kitchen Range was evolved with the Shaker and Tall Storage Jar. The Shaker was in the style of a saltcellar and was 5" tall, 2" across the top and 3¼" across the base. Most of the Shakers had 'Flour', 'Salt', or 'Sugar', painted over the decoration. The Tall Storage Jars usually had 'Tea', or 'Coffee', painted over the decoration. These jars were supplied with a lid. One that was called 'Mops and Things' was supplied without the lid. The Shaker mould was also used to produce a small table lamp. A large hole was made in the top to accommodate the light fitting and a hole drilled in the side, close to the base, for the electric cable. Several of these table lamps were made but it is not known if they were ever offered for sale to the general public.

A small dish that was added to the kitchen range was 3" in diameter, 2" deep and supplied with a lid. Most of these had "Brillo" painted across the decoration and were generally known as such.

'Face pots' were in fashion for a little while and included 'Celery', 'Spring Onion', 'Beetroot', and 'Apple Sauce' among them. Some were stamped with the Dragon mark and some with Dee Cee. The 'face pot' idea was originally designed by Sylvac Pottery but numerous other potteries have produced copies, or used the ideas in designing their own products, and Dragon was no exception. The Sylvac pottery was in production from 1894 until 1982.

Novelty pots were introduced during the 1970's in an attempt to boost sales. These included a Piggy Bank in the form of a small pig, and a Hen which was in two pieces and similar to the one featured in the BBC series of 'Bread' in 1986.

The Welsh honey industry was a very good customer of Dragon. In the 1975 Holgate Honey, of Aberaeron, approached Dragon with a view to obtaining a small pot which could be filled with honey. This is what is usually referred to as a kitchen storage jar with lid. These pots were quite costly, and slow, to produce due to the time taken to apply the decoration. As a result of this Holgate requested an additional smaller jar which could be produced more quickly, and cheaply. The pot chosen was 2½" in diameter and 2½" tall. The lid featured a flower with four petals, in relief, which was repeated four times around the sides. These pots were glazed with a transparent brown, green, or blue glaze. This did not denote a different type of honey but simply made the retailer's display look more attractive. Holgate specified that the base of the pot and the underside of the lid were not to be glazed. This was achieved by painting these areas with wax before the glaze was applied. After Holgate filled the pots with honey they were sealed with a visk-ring. This was a plastic ring which was put on wet then, as it dried out, it shrank sealing the pot.

Another Welsh honey company, details of which are not known, also approached Dragon in the 1970's. They requested that a small pot, with lid, be made, and to cost as little as possible. The result was a little like a miniature version of the marmalade pot. It is possible that only sufficient for one season's honey output was produced, whereas those for Holgate were produced for a number of years.

Besides the standard products, which have been described above, a number of experimental, and very low volume of production items, were made from time to time. Photographs of some of these can be found in the Product Gallery.

Production Processes

Manufacturing

The Clay

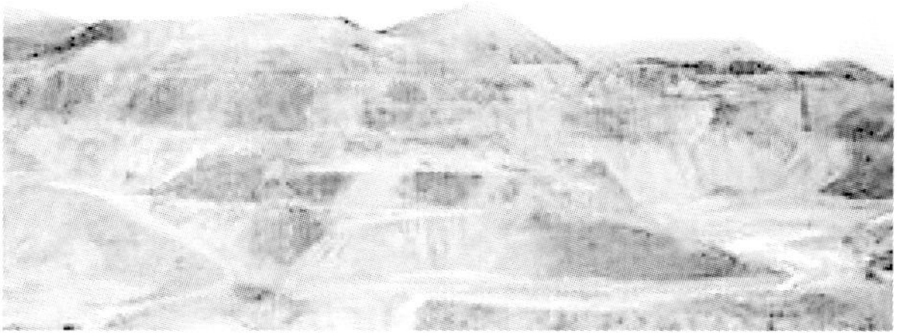

This originated from the large china clay deposits still to be found in Cornwall, where it was partly refined before being transported, in bulk, to be further processed by specialist companies in the Stoke on Trent area. The processed clay was then packed into plastic bags, each containing 56lbs, and delivered by road to Rhayader.

The clay, which was used initially, produced a pot that was white when it had been fired. In about 1971, this was changed to one that produced a pot with a pale cream colour, although variations have been observed ranging from 'almost white' through to 'rich cream'.

Making the Pots

Thrown Method – 1962 to 1971

This is the method used by traditional potters where a piece of clay of a suitable size is placed on the centre of the wheel. The artistic hands, and fingers, of the potter transform the clay into the desired rounded shape while the wheel is turning. When the desired shape has been achieved the potter passes a cutting wire under the base of the pot to separate it from the wheel. Great care is needed to lift the pot and place it in a safe place to dry out.

If a handle needs to be attached, or a pouring lip formed, this is carried out when the pot has dried to the leather-hard state, also known as 'Greenware', and is still pliable. With table lamps this is also the time when a hole is drilled in the side of the base for the electrical cable to be passed through.

When the pot has dried to the white-hard state it is ready to be fettled in readiness for the biscuit firing.

At Dragon, the potters did not usually place the piece of clay directly on to the wheel but onto a piece of asbestos, or hardboard type of material, which had already been attached to the wheel. This avoided the need for the potter to handle the delicate piece when placing it aside to start its drying process.

Slipcasting – 1964 to 1982

This is the modern method of pottery production used to produce items on a large scale and of consistent size and quality.

The method was used from about 1964 on a very small scale in the old pottery. Its use was steadily built up during the early days of the new pottery and in about 1971, when 'throwing' ceased, 'slipcasting' became the main method employed. As its name implies it used 'slip' and moulds in which the product was cast.

'Slip' is the name given to the liquid clay which is used in this process. The clay is the same as that used for the thrown method except that it is mixed with water until it has the consistency of cream. This mixing takes place in a large vessel fitted with rotating paddles, a little like a butter churn, sometimes called a 'blunger'.

With slipcasting the fine art of the traditional potter is lost and replaced by the art of the pattern maker. It is he who makes the master models from which the moulds are made. These are casts made with plaster of Paris and for a typical vase, or something similar, there would normally be three sections – two sides and a base, sometimes referred to as a foot.

The sections of the plaster mould are carefully assembled and the slip poured in until it reaches the top of the mould. The thickness of the cast pot depends on the length of time which the slip is in the mould and the rate at which the plaster can absorb moisture. At Dragon, this was about ten minutes after which the remaining liquid slip was poured out to be used again.

When the remaining liquid slip has been poured out the clay which remains is quite solid and is in the shape of the desired pot but is not strong enough to support itself.

After standing for an hour or two, during which more moisture is absorbed by the plaster of Paris, the clay shrinks a little and becomes stronger. When this has happened the sections of the mould are removed to reveal the pot. As with the thrown method this is the time when any handles are attached, pouring lips formed or holes drilled. The pot is then left for some hours to dry out further until it is white-hard, 'whiteware', and ready to be fettled prior to being biscuit fired and decorated.

The sections of the mould are also allowed to dry out before being used again.

With care, it is possible to re-use a set of moulds many times before it has to be discarded and replaced with a new one.

A set of moulds would be discarded if it was damaged, especially where one section mated up with another, or if the surface had become clogged with the very fine particles of clay resulting in the absorption ability of the plaster being greatly diminished.

For each design, there would be a large number of sets in stock either in use or drying out ready for the next time.

When new moulds were required, it was usually Mr Cornish, or one of his expert assistants, who carried out this work although, if it was a very busy period, the work would be passed to a specialist company in the Potteries.

Press Moulding

When the throwing method was being phased out this method was introduced to produce the traditional plant-pot and its associated saucer.

The press was heavy piece of equipment consisting of an inner and an outer mould made of metal, an hydraulic cylinder to provide the pressure, and an electric motor to turn one of the moulds.

The surfaces of the moulds, which came into contact with the clay, were lightly oiled before a large piece of clay was placed into the outer mould. Power was switched on and the inner mould lowered into place with hydraulic pressure so that the pot was formed. At the same time, the electric power was used to turn the moulds so that the metal of the mould slid on the clay ensuring that the surface of the pot was smooth.

After the pot was removed from the press, it was given a light firing to burn off any oil that might be on the surface and then left to dry before being fettled and then decorated.

The clay that was used in this process was usually the waste clay which had been processed by the pug mill.

This clay could have been derived from faulty output of slipcasting, or other sources of hard clay, either fired or just dry, which had then been reduced to powder in a crusher.

Pot Base Design

From the time that production first started every pot that was produced on the wheel featured a smooth base, as did early production of most of the slipcast products, and plant pots produced by the press method.

This caused a problem in that when the pot was glazed the base became covered, together with the rest of the pot. If it had been placed in the kiln, and fired, the pot would have adhered to the tray. After firing, both would have been damaged when they were separated. To overcome this problem the base of every pot was rubbed on a scouring pad, a piece of thick wet felt, or similar product, to remove this unwanted glaze.

Eventually, all of the moulds for the slipcast pots, that featured a smooth base, were altered so that a 'footring' was formed as an integral part of the pot. Incorporating the footring meant that glaze only had to be removed from a very small area.

The Salt and Pepper were not affected by this glazing problem, to the same extent, due to the fact that they were cast in the inverted position. The lid of the mould incorporated a large hole through which the slip was poured. The lid was removed after the surplus slip had been poured out to reveal what was to become the base complete with the recessed hole to accommodate the rubber or plastic stopper. This, in effect, gave the pots the necessary footring, but meant that it was not possible to apply the back stamp.

The Mustard Pot appears to be a pot on which an attempt was made to incorporate 'Made in Wales', in relief, in the centre of the recess when the footring was being formed. I have seen one very good example of this , and another where it has almost been worn away but is still decipherable. This latter example dates from 1979, or later. In both cases the recess was too rough for the back stamp to be applied. The majority of Mustard Pots was produced with a smooth recess and the use of the back stamp.

Another pot on which a trial was made was the Bulb Bowl. In this case a 'mould size (or reference)' was impressed into the recess. I have seen two examples of the 7 inch diameter bowl, one with 'NO I' and the other with 'No 1', together with a report of a 'No 3' on a bowl of 8½ inch diameter.

Pug Mill

A pug mill is, basically, a very large mincing machine which is used to mix clay into a more homogeneous state.

Waste clay is fed into the hopper where it meets up with a worm feed. This forces the clay through the cutters where it is broken into small pieces. From here it passes into a vacuum chamber to remove any air which might be present, and then is forced down a tapered barrel from which it emerges as a continuous piece of clay. This is then cut into suitable lengths ready for further use.

The output from the mill was usually destined for the press, but could also be used to produce slip, if required.

Fettling

Each pot is fettled when it is in the white-hard state, before being fired, and is strong enough to stand being handled.

Fettling is the term used to describe the removal of any casting seams and to the general cleaning of the pots using a fettling knife, scraper, sandpaper or any other suitable implement or material, before being finally washed to remove any remaining dust particles. It can be quite a dusty process so great care is needed with regards to the health of the workers.

Firing

Kilns

When all of the production had finally been moved to the new building, there were two trolley kilns, three medium kilns and four small kilns in regular use. All were electrically heated and were usually switched on in the early evening to take advantage of the off-peak overnight electricity tariff.

Temperature Control

The temperature in the trolley kilns was controlled automatically through the use of timers and temperature sensors.

The temperature in the oven kilns was monitored by observing the 'cones', which were placed at a slight angle close to the inspection hole. These cones were small pyramids of compressed glaze materials, which softened and bent over at certain temperatures. Usually there were three cones in a group, one to bend over just below the required temperature, one to bend when the required temperature had been reached and a third one to indicate that the temperature was too high and that overfiring was happening.

Biscuit Firing

The purpose of biscuit firing is to remove all moisture from the product and to fuse the mineral elements of the clay together to give the product sufficient strength to be a durable product. Without this firing the product would be very brittle.

This firing usually took 12 to 14 hours, depending upon the size of the kiln. For about the first 2 hours the temperature was set to ‘low’ in order to slowly evaporate any moisture still remaining in the clay, otherwise the pot might have exploded and damaged other pots at the same time. The controls were then set for the temperature to rise steadily until 1100°C was reached. The quality of the pot was dependent on the temperature, and the time taken to reach it, so that the various minerals, which were present in the clay, fused together correctly. When the firing was complete, the power was switched off and everything allowed to cool down slowly. Towards the end of the cooling period the doors were opened and the remaining heat allowed to circulate. When the pots were cool enough they were then placed on shelves to await decoration.

Glaze, or Glost, Firing

This firing takes place after the decoration has been completed and the protective coat of glaze has been applied.

The purpose of this firing is to fuse the glaze into a glass-like surface which seals the microscopic pores on the surface of the product to prevent the absorption of any moisture, or other matter, to protect any decoration, and to make the product fully serviceable.

This firing would usually take less time than the biscuit firing and to the slightly lower temperature of about 1030°C.

Power would normally be switched on for about 12 hours from 6pm to about 6am. The kilns would then be allowed to cool slowly. Towards lunchtime the doors would be opened a little and then opened a little more at intervals so that by the end of the day the fired pots would be cool enough to handle and place on the storage shelves in readiness to be packed and despatched.

Decorating

Decoration, with very few exceptions, involved painting with underglaze colours. These colours, which came in the form of powder, were mixed with water in very precise quantities. If these quantities were not adhered to then the shade of colour achieved would be wrong. In order to maintain the correct shade the painter also had to ensure that the mix was stirred each time the brush was refilled. This was to prevent the particles of colour falling out of the suspension and forming a solid mass in the bottom of the container.

The main piece of equipment used by the painter was a workbench fitted with a revolving table, which could be operated by hand, or by a foot treadle underneath. The workpiece was placed in the centre of the table and each colour applied in turn.

Ann Pugh

Christine Nicholls

All the styles of decoration, which involved the use of paint, were carried out before the glaze was applied. Because the pot was very porous, each application of colour dried very quickly, leaving a fragile layer of colour residue on the surface of the pot.

Six basic styles of decoration were used on products: -

a) Horizontal bands of colour.
b) Wide vertical brush strokes.
c) Mottled effect.
d) All-over coloured glaze.
e) All-over lustre glaze
f) Applied transfers.

Horizontal Bands

The most common, and popular, style of decoration for which Dragon is so easily recognised is the application of bands of colour. These are mainly autumn colours of green, brown, sepia and yellow, together with shade variations.

Yellow was usually used as a background colour. When it was used, it was the first colour to be applied to the pot. With all of the colours, there were various shades.

From about 1966 ranges were produced in either blue, black, or turquoise, and not usually in conjunction with any other colour.

All pots, except fruit dishes and other small dishes, had their main decoration on the outside. With regards to these exceptions, the bands were applied mainly to the inside in the form of concentric circles. The outside was usually decorated with one or two shallow bands.

In most cases, the number of bands applied depended on the height of the pot and the final aesthetic appearance of the finished product.

When the paint had dried, the pot was ready to have the intricate designs applied to the colour bands. At Dragon, this process was always known as 'etching', although many people refer to it as 'sgraffito'.

The tools used for etching were usually homemade by each of the artists and might be fashioned from sharpened nails, or a piece of bamboo, or a pin, or needle, mounted in a holding device. Anything which the artist was comfortable in using, and which also enabled her to produce the desired result on the pot, was used.

For pots produced as a holiday souvenirs, to advertise a company, or to commemorate an event, the appropriate inscription was etched into one of the colour bands.

With regards to 'kitchen' items such as Sugar, Flour, Tea, Brillo, etc, these names were usually painted in black after the rest of the decoration had been completed.

In the case of the 'Brown Leaf' design for Dee Cee, this was painted over the colour band(s). The etching tool was used to define the veins of the leaf and to highlight the outer edges.

In the mid 1970's as costs rose dramatically with inflation, a demand for a lower priced pot was identified. This was satisfied by producing a pot without the etching with the result that costs and prices could be held down and production throughput increased.

Wide Vertical Brush Strokes

As the heading implies this was the use of wide brush strokes to cover the pot in a series of broad vertical lines of colour. The colours, which were usually associated with this style of decoration, were shades of pale greens, browns and yellows. Very rarely was any wide band left unpainted between the colours.

Mottled Effect

Sponge, instead of brushes, was used to create this effect. Brown, green and yellow were the colours normally used.

The technique was usually, first of all, to cover the whole of the decorative area of the pot with a thinned-down pale yellow. This had the effect of providing a pale background colour as well as sealing the pores of the pot.

The next stage was to apply the remaining colours. This was achieved by impregnating a small piece of sponge with the brown, or green, colour and then lightly, dabbing the pot with a slight twisting action to give a swirl effect. The fact that the surface had been made smooth, with the yellow, helped to give the apparent thickness variations of colour to the finished product.

All-over Coloured Glaze

Transparent coloured glaze was usually used on pots that incorporated a design in relief, including the basket in which the HEN sat, and does not appear to have been used in association with other methods of decoration.

Opaque coloured glaze was used to decorate one range that was all-over mustard in colour, and there may have been others.

All-over Lustre Glaze

For a short period a few pot designs were finished in a silver lustre, or a gun metal lustre.

So far only the egg cup, bulb bowl, jug, candle holder and a bowl incorporating a cube shaped base, have been observed.

When this type of glaze has been used it is not possible to show the usual back stamp. This was overcome, at least on the jug, by attaching a pre-printed paper label to the base after firing.

Applied Transfers

This is a method of applying decoration to a pot without the need for very much artistic talent, just a steady hand and a sharp eye.

The transfers, which were printed on thin paper, were moistened with water and then placed on the pot, which had previously been glazed. The transfer was then manipulated into the correct position, any bubbles of air or excess water being removed by gentle dabbing before the backing paper was discarded.

The finished pot was finally given a light firing, at about 800°C , to set the colours.

Staff Photographs

Mr and Mrs Cornish

Some of the workers at Mr and Mrs Cornish's Pottery in Rhayader. From the left they are: Nineteen-year-old Carol Lawton, a product of Birmingham art school and college; Ann Thomas, 18, from Llanwrthwl, who "thinks of everything" about the pottery; asbestos-gloved Veronica Dowding, 18, removing hot "pots" from one of the small kilns with 16-year-old Philip Lumsden; Mrs Jill Fenner and Phyllis Hedges hand-painting designs.

1963

1969

John
Hancock

Tom
Griffiths

Eileen
Davis

Philip
Lumsden

Joyce ?

Mrs
Hedges

?

Pat
Thomas

Mrs
Cornish

Harold
Turner

Mr
Cornish

Mrs
Futcher

Eirwen
Davis

Retirement of Mrs Futcher in August 1979

Tom
Griffiths

Gail
Davis

Heather
Jarman

Ken
Jackaman

Edith
Jackaman

Christine
Nicholls

Peter
Sherwood

Mrs
Futcher

Betty
Thomas

Ernest
Husson

Ann
Albiston
(see below)

Steve
Reynolds

Marshall
Jones

Ron
Johnson

Ann
Pugh

Nicki
Johnson

Mrs
Brookes

Mrs Cornish did not like to have two girls with the same name so Ann Albiston was known as ‘Wendy’.

PRODUCT GALLERY

Dear Reader / Collector,

On the following pages you will see over 300 photographs of Dragon products with their variation of decoration.

Somewhere, out there in collections, there must be items from the early pre-slipcast days, which I have not seen, and therefore have not been recorded in the history of Dragon.

Although the portrayal of slipcast products is almost complete the record of decoration styles for particular items is not. This is especially so in respect of the Mottled, Rainbow, Vertical Stripes and Coloured Glaze ranges.

Many items commemorating an event, incorporating a place name, or a commercial enterprise, were produced in small numbers from about 1965. They were usually of a very local nature and are now rare items worthy of inclusion into the history.

I am also looking for photographs of the sitting HEN which was made in the 1970's. Many variations of this subject have been made by many potteries over the years, and are still being made to this day. The one that I am looking for, and there are most likely variations in decoration, must have the genuine Dragon backstamp on the base.

If any reader can send me any photograph, preferably digital via email, of any missing item then I would be very grateful.

Provided that sufficient new material becomes available I hope to eventually produce a second edition in which recognition will be given to all new contributors.

Product Gallery - Contents

Thistle Vase - Tall

Height 7½ inches - Slipcast

Thistle Vase - Tall (Cont)

(karina8573)

(alfiec)

(julezx)

(debdusantiques)

Dee Cee

Thistle Vase - Medium

Height 4¾ inches - Thrown

(earlybirds1)

(ithell)

(suesdogo)
Dee Cee

Thistle Vase - Medium

Height 4¾ inches - Slipcast

(alfiec)

Thistle Vase - Small

Height 3½ inches - Slipcast

Thistle Vase – Small (Cont)

(zaynee_jaynee)

Dee Cee

(singingpostman)

Dee Cee

Tall Slim Vase

Height as indicated - Slipcast

6 inches

6 inches

8 inches

(rainbow-antiques)
8 inches

(younglad25)
8 inches

Barrel Vase - Tall

Height 9 inches - Slipcast

(linda3335)

(connie1313cat)

(recyclane)

(2dandy4)

Barrel Vase - Medium

Height as indicated - Thrown

(alonewolfhound)

5¼ inches

(debdusantiques)

4½ inches

Dee Cee

4¼ inches

Dee Cee

4¾ inches

Barrel Vase - Medium

Height 4½ inches - Slipcast

(fiftiescollectables)

(ceef169)

Barrel Vase - Small

Height 3 inches - Slipcast

Dee Cee

Dee Cee

Dee Cee

Round Vase

Height 3 inches - diameter 3¼ inches - Slipcast

(celfletch)

Dee Cee

The lidded version has, so far, only been seen in the Rainbow colours (lower right) and all-over blue.

Miscellaneous Vases

Various heights from 7 to 12 inches, and thrown, except where stated

(tammye177)

Dee Cee
4¼ inches

Slipcast
3 inches
Mini Thistle Vase

Rose Bowl - Large

Height (excluding lid) 4 inches - overall diameter 7 inches

Slipcast

Rose Bowl - Small

Height (excluding lid) 4 inches - overall diameter 4½ inches

Slipcast

Crocus Bowl

Height 4 inches - Slipcast

(5uperwoman54)

Bulb Bowl Large

Diameter 9 inches approx.

Slipcast

(crystalfm)

(trish711)

(hopper485)

(chrome-girl)

Dee Cee

(marley202)

Dee Cee

Bulb Bowl Small

Height 3½ inches - overall diameter 7 inches

Slipcast

(suesdogo)

Dee Cee

Round Bowl

Heights various - 2 ½ to 4 inches - thrown

(fiftiescollectables)

Round Bowl (Cont)

Round Bowl (Cont)

(singingpostman)

All five items are '**Dee Cee**' brand

Round Bowl

Height 3½ Inches - Slipcast

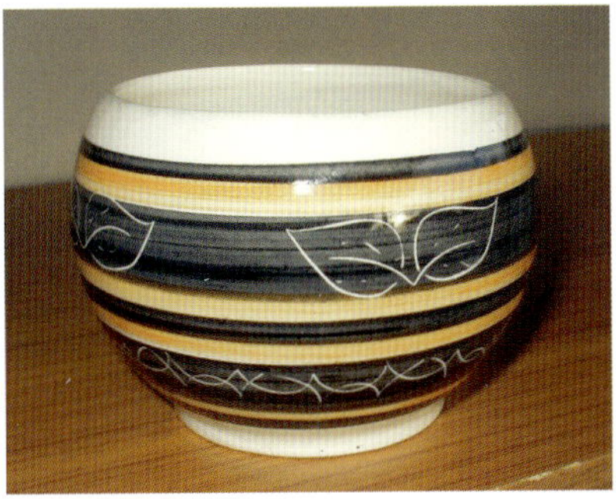

Dee Cee

Planter "Heavyweight" - Large

Height 5½ inches - diameter 6 inches

Slipcast

(hazel-r-j)

Dee Cee

Planter "Heavyweight" - Medium

Height 4½ inches - diameter 5¼ inches

Slipcast

Planter "Lightweight" - Large

Height 7½ inches - diameter 9 inches

Slipcast

Planter "Lightweight" - Medium

Height 4½ inches - diameter 6½ inches

Slipcast

Planter "Fluted"

Height 4½ inches – diameter 5½ inches

Slipcast

Plant Pot

Thrown

Height 4 inches - diameter 5 inches

Plant Pot

Height 5 inches - diameter 6 inches

Press Moulded

A typical saucer usually supplied with each plant pot

Plant Pot

Height 4 inches - diameter 5 inches

Press Moulded

Dee Cee

Jugs - Various

Thrown

Height 4 inches

Height 3½ inches

Height 4 inches approx

Height 4 inches approx

Jugs - Traditional

(Sometimes referred to as 'Sparrowbeak')

Height – Many variations ranging from 4 inches to 7 ½ inches

Slipcast

Jugs – Traditional (Cont)

Dee Cee

(sophie1230)

Dee Cee

(yehsur)

(frj346)

Dee Cee

Jugs - Mint Sauce etc

Height 3 inches - Slipcast

Mint Sauce for
Welsh Lamb

(steptoeandson)

(earlybirds1)

Severn Bridge

(derryclay)

Drinking Mug

Height 4½ inches

Thrown

Drinking Mug

Slipcast

(5uperwoman54

(simon4uk)

Dee Cee

Tankard

Height 4 inches - Slipcast

(ibiza48)

(golfwatch1)

Tankard (Cont)

(jillytiques)

(dunbooting)

(pete2480)

(thepickypeddler)

Tankard (Cont)

(Jackcousins)

(rhinoceros_101)

(springyrich)

Goblet

Height 4¾ inches - slipcast

Egg Separator

Height 2½ inches - Slipcast

(fiftiescollectables)

(pandoragardening)

Brillo

Height (excluding lid) 2 inches - diameter 3 inches

Slipcast

(partime_ratty)

(me123cars)

Storage Jars

Height (excluding lid) 4½ inches - Slipcast

(earlybirds1)

(louscupboard)
No lid supplied

(sophielocks)

Shaker

Height 5 inches - diameter of base 3½ inches

Slipcast

(hazel-r-j)

Kitchen & Ovenware

Slipcast

Depth 3 inches - diameter 6 inches

Depth 2 inches - diameter 3¾ inches

Depth 3¼ inches - top 7½ x 5½ inches

Depth 4 inches - diameter 6 inches

Depth 2¼ inches - diameter 3 inches

Kitchen & Ovenware (Cont)

Height 7½ inches

Height 5½ inches

Face Pots

Height 4¾ inches and 6 inches - Slipcast

Note - These designs were introduced to Dragon by Dee Cee. Previously they had been produced by West Country Pottery for Dee Cee. Both styles are to be found with either the Dragon stamp or Dee Cee.

Tea Pot

Slipcast

Teapot Stand

Slipcast

Tea Strainer Basin

Height 1¾ inches - overall diameter 3½ inches

Slipcast

Coffee Pot

Slipcast

Dee Cee (spendalotlil)

Milk and Sugar

Milk - Height 3½ inches - Slipcast
Sugar - Height 2½ inches - Slipcast

Salt and Pepper

Slipcast

Initial Design

This was the first design of the Salt and Pepper. It was most likely the first use of slipcasting by Dragon and was introduced in about 1964. The design was of slimmer proportions than the one which replaced it in 1966. This later design range also included the Vinegar and Mustard.

Height 5¼ ins

Salt and Pepper (Cont)

Subsequent Design

The first production was 5¾ to 6 inches tall. This was in order to match the corresponding Vinegar. A little later a demand was identified for a slightly smaller version which resulted in one being 4¾ to 5 inches tall.

Dee Cee

Dee Cee

Dee Cee

(tucktonbelle)
Dee Cee

All of the above examples are 5¾ to 6 inches tall.

Salt and Pepper (Cont)

All of the above examples are 4¾ to 5 inches tall.

Height 3 inches

Mustard Pot

Height (excluding lid) 2½ inches - overall width 2¾ inches

Slipcast

(the_mini_man)

Dee Cee

Dee Cee

Dee Cee

Vinegar / Vignarette

Height 6 inches - Slipcast

(y4knlnotz)

Dee Cee

Dee Cee

(jenny900)

Dee Cee

Marmalade / Preserve Pot

Height (excluding lid) 3¾ inches approx.

Thrown

(ownsweb)

(redsmithy101)

Dee Cee

Marmalade / Preserve Pot

Height (excluding lid) 3¾ inches - overall diameter 4¾ inches

Slipcast

Missing lid

Dee Cee (simon4uk)
Missing Lid

This example has had the gold added by a previous owner

Marmalade / Preserve Pot

Height (excluding lid) 2¾ inches - overall diameter 3¾ inches

Slipcast

(katescollectables)

Dee Cee (debdusantiques)

Egg Cup

Height 2½ inches - Slipcast

Beetroot

Height (excluding lid) 3½ inches

Slipcast

This style of pot was sometimes referred to as 'Beetroot' because of the shape of the lid and knob, even though there was no wording present.

(5uperwoman54)

(flashgordon7770)

Butter Dish

Height (excluding lid) 2 inches - overall diameter 5½ inches

Slipcast

(s900t)

Dee Cee

Traditional Cheese / Butter

Length 9 inches - Width 4 inches

Slipcast

(recyclaine)

(steptoeandson777)

(murraymints)

(sophielocks)

Jam Dish

Dee Cee

Thrown - Base 2¾ and top 5 inches in diameter
- Height 1½ inches

Slipcast - Base 3¼ and top 4¾ inches in diameter
- Height 1 inch

Slipcast (bobf192)

Dee Cee

Fruit Dish

Diameters vary from 7 inches to 10 inches

Majority of examples have been thrown

(purplebear69)

(caesarphil)
Dee Cee

(emporium0_1)
Dee Cee

(sixtiesladz)
Dee Cee

(theredditchcollector)
Dee Cee

Table Lamp - Beehive

Heights vary between 6 inches and 9½ inches

The majority was thrown, although a mould was made for slipcasting when the thrown method was discontinued. The slipcast items can be identified by a smooth 'inside' to the body, and, as in the case illustrated, only the later styles of decoration were applied.

Being large items, as well as being thrown, styles have varied considerably over the period. Only one style was made using the slipcast method.

(steve8lou)

Table Lamp – Beehive (Cont)

Dee Cee

Dee Cee

Dee Cee

(caizer22)

Dee Cee

(leatherlacecat)

Slipcast
(later style of decoration)

Table Lamps - Other

'Tia Maria' Bottle Shape

Height 5 inches - Thrown

Dee Cee

Tall Lamp

Heights vary from 8 inches to 12+ inches - Thrown

Dee Cee

Table Lamps - Other (Cont)

Tall Barrel Vase Lamp

Height 9½ inches - Slipcast

Experimental

Based on the Shaker

Based on the Salt and Pepper

Note:
Some table lamps do exist which are based on an inverted Tall Thistle Vase.

Bon Bon Dish

Height 2 inches - Maximum diameter 5½ inches

Slipcast

Dee Cee (earlybirds1)

Pin / Trinket Dish

Height 1¼ inches – base diameter range 2¾ to 3½ inches
top diameter 4½ to 5 inches depending on degree of fluting

Slipcast

Pin / Trinket Dish (Cont)

(caizer22)

(lehlooe)

Dee Cee

Dee Cee

Sundry Small Dishes

Diameter 5¼ inches
Dee Cee

(artocrat333)
Diameter 4¾ inches

Diameter 3½ inches

(ttocsnomis)
Diameter 3½ inches

Holgate Honey

Slipcast
Specially produced for Holgate Honey Farm, Aberaeron.

Height (excluding lid) 3¾ inches

(Halo foods, Tywyn)

(ownsweb)

Height (excluding lid) 2¼ inches – also produced in blue

Miscellaneous Containers

3¼ x 3¼ ins
Lidded Pot

Height 2¼ ins (excl lid)
Made for a Welsh Honey Producer

Dee Cee

Dee Cee

Other Miscellaneous

Piggy Bank

Steak Plate

Unusual Bowl
Diameter 7 inches (wonder66)

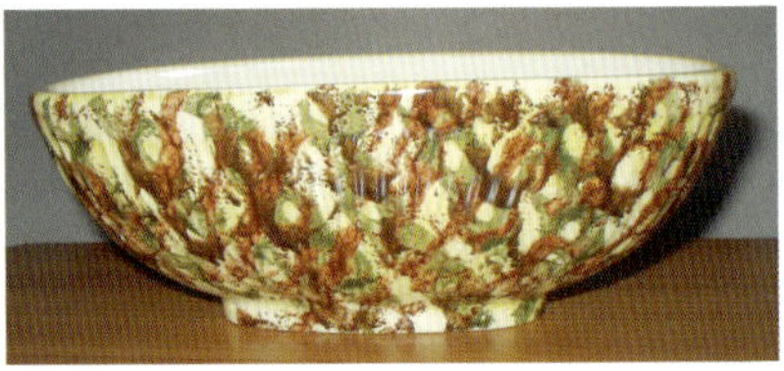

Fluted Trough - Length 8 inches

(reelukabb1938)
Candle Holder
4½ tall 3¼ square

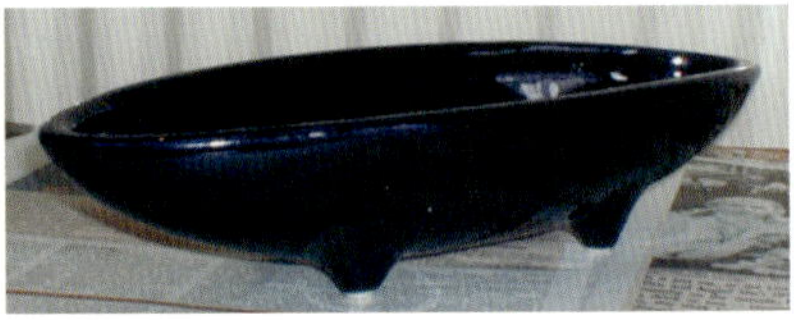

Trough, also referred to as a 'Boat'. It was made in two sizes, 11 inches and 17 inches in length, and three colours. blue, green, and white.

Back Stamps

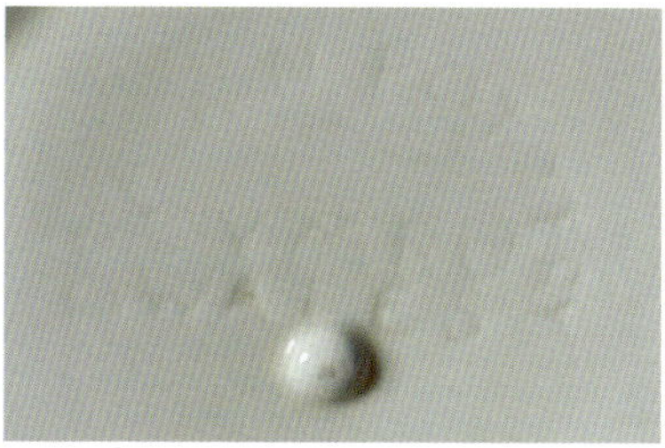

DRAGON POTTERY
MADE
IN
WALE
RHAYADER

DRAGON POTTERY
WALES
RHAYADER

MADE
IN
WALES

DRAGON POTTERY
MADE
IN
WALES
RHAYADER

DRAGON POTTERY
MADE
IN
WALES
RHAYADER

DRAGON POTTERY
MADE
IN
WALES
RHAYADER

No.1

NO.1

Dee - Cee
made
in Wales